Made in The South Pacific

Christine Price

MADE IN THE SOUTH PACIFIC

Arts of the Sea People

illustrated with photographs and drawings

E. P. DUTTON   NEW YORK

This book is for Jean,
in Samoa and New Mexico

LIBRARY OF CONGRESS CATALOGING IN PUBLICATION DATA

Price, Christine, date   Made in the South Pacific.

SUMMARY: *Describes the arts of the people of the Pacific islands both in the past and today.*
1. Art—Islands of the Pacific—Juvenile literature.
2. Art, Primitive—Islands of the Pacific—Juvenile literature. [1. Art—Islands of the Pacific.
2. Art, Primitive—Islands of the Pacific.
3. Islands of the Pacific] I. Title.
N7410.P74   709'.01'1   78-12807   ISBN: 0-525-34397-0

Published in the United States by E. P. Dutton, a Division of Sequoia-Elsevier Publishing Company, Inc., New York

Published simultaneously in Canada by Clarke, Irwin & Company Limited, Toronto and Vancouver

Editor: Ann Troy   Designer: Riki Levinson

Printed in the U.S.A.   First Edition
10 9 8 7 6 5 4 3 2 1

Illustration page i: Wooden stopper for gourd container. Santa Cruz Islands. Frontispiece: Detail of carving at end of a carrying pole. Hawaii.

Author's Note

Working on this book has been a voyage of discovery, impossible to make without help along the way.

I am deeply grateful to the authors whose works introduced me to Pacific arts and cultures. Some of these books, especially those richly illustrated, appear in the list of *Books for Further Reading*. I also owe a great debt to the people in the South Pacific, the United States and England, who helped me so generously during my travels and research. They have provided encouragement, shared their knowledge and opened up for me new and exciting views of Pacific art and life.

My special thanks are due to the following, for supplying me with photographs and granting permission to include them in the book:

The American Museum of Natural History, New York; James Barker; The Bernice P. Bishop Museum, Honolulu; The Trustees of the British Museum, London; The Brooklyn Museum, New York; W. K. Curtis; Philip J. C. Dark; The Field Museum of Natural History, Chicago; Charles Hunt, former Director of the Fiji Museum; The La Trobe Collection, State Library of Victoria, Melbourne; Nancy Lutton, Librarian, New Guinea Collection, University of Papua New Guinea; The Ministry of Information, Fiji; The Otago Museum, Dunedin, New Zealand; Hera Owen, Director of the Palau Museum; The Peabody Museum, Harvard University; The Peabody Museum of Salem, Massachusetts; Eric

Wooden ceremonial sword inlaid with shell. Palau, Caroline Islands.

M. Saville; The UCLA Museum of Cultural History, Los Angeles; The United Nations; The University Museum, University of Pennsylvania.

The poem, "Song of Hiro," quoted on page 14, is from *Ancient Tahiti* by Teuira Henry, B. P. Bishop Bulletin, no. 48, 1928, p. 550. It is included by kind permission of the Bishop Museum Press.

Finally I am particularly grateful to Dr. Roland Force and Mr. Marvin Montvel-Cohen for their careful readings of the manuscript and helpful comments and criticisms. They are naturally not responsible for any errors that may remain.

The subject of this book is as vast as the South Pacific itself. Like the sea peoples of old, I have launched out on great waters. I hope that some readers will want to go beyond the horizon of these pages and make new discoveries and fresh landfalls for themselves.

C. P.
New Mexico

Above: Drum. Papuan Gulf.
Opposite: Gourd container.
Trobriand Islands.

Contents

MICRONESIA

Hawaiian Islands

Guam

Yap Is.

Caroline Islands

Palau Is.

Ponape

Marshall Islands

Mortlock Islands

Kosrae

Gilbert Islands

Admiralty
Islands

New Ireland

Marquesas Islands

PAPUA
NEW GUINEA

Trobriand
Islands

Solomon Islands

Santa Cruz Islands

Samoa

Society Islands

Torres
Strait

Papuan Gulf

Bellona

New
Hebrides

Espiritu Santo

Fiji

Tonga

Cook
Islands

Tahiti

AUSTRALIA

New
Caledonia

Lau Islands

Rarotonga

MELANESIA

Austral Islands

NEW
ZEALAND

POLYNESIA

Map of The

BAIA
CALIFORNIA

Easter Island •

outh Pacific

1

People
of the Canoe

The seafaring canoes of the South Pacific will be our guides to the arts of the island peoples. In their canoes the ancient seafarers launched out to settle the hundreds of islands scattered over the blue spaces of the sea—islands large and small, high and low; lush green islands and dry, windswept atolls of white coral sand.

Without seaworthy vessels, shaped to move with wind and wave and commanded by bold navigators, there could be no exploring or settlement of the vast world of the South Pacific. The islands lay waiting for the sea people, the people of the canoe, for whom the sea was not a barrier but a highway, leading eastward toward the rising sun.

Opposite: Hawaiian double canoe, 1777.
Above: Wood-carved dolphin.
Eastern Solomon Islands.

The first comers to the South Pacific islands, more than 25,000 years ago, were dark-skinned people from the southeast coast of Asia. They settled on the great mountainous landmass of New Guinea, which lies at the western gateway of the Pacific. Gradually they spread into the clusters of islands to the north and east, and the lands they settled have come to be known as Melanesia, the Islands of Black People.

The migration of these Melanesian seafarers must have lasted for many generations before they finally pushed eastward as far as Fiji. They were a varied stream of peoples, speaking a number of different languages. The settlers on each island group developed their own lifeways, arts, and ceremonies and their own forms of canoes. Small, slender outrigger canoes were for fishing and traveling along the coast. Large vessels, like the mighty *ndrua* of Fiji or the *lakatoi* of New Guinea, were designed for long trading voyages or for raids on other islands in time of war.

Some of the Melanesians moved northward from New Guinea into Micronesia—the Small Islands. There a canoe might travel for weeks without a landfall, and many islands were so low-lying that they could easily pass by unseen. Only the most skillful navigators could survive and make those seas their highway. Yet 4,000 years ago settlers came there from the Philippines and Indonesia, bold sailors of outrigger canoes. Their descendants in Micronesia built the swiftest canoes in the Pacific and developed a wonderful system of navigation.

Opposite: Lakatoi *under sail. Port Moresby, Papua New Guinea, 1885.*

2

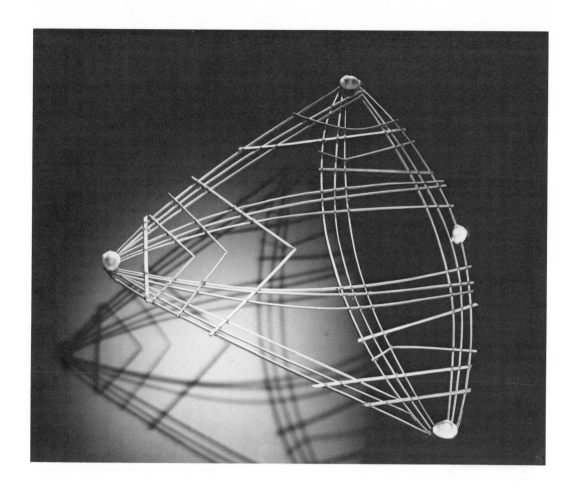

The art of the navigator was passed down from father to son in the form of secret songs and chants. Canoe captains used magic spells to ward off storms at sea, but their navigation was firmly based on knowledge of stars and cloud forms, the flyways of birds, and the direction of prevailing winds.

Among the flat atolls of the Marshall Islands, the navigator studied the movements of the water beneath his canoe. The set of the ocean currents and swells told him of the presence of unseen land. This knowledge was recorded in stick charts. These were diagrams of the movements of the sea around the groups of islands, represented on the chart by white cowrie shells.

Opposite: Beached canoe. Marshall Islands.
Above: Stick chart. Utric Atoll,
Marshall Islands.

East of Micronesia there was only empty sea, but beyond Fiji lay new lands to be discovered, the vast world of Polynesia—the Many Islands. The explorers and settlers of Polynesia may possibly have come from the coasts of southern China about 2000 B.C., but the story of their origin is still not clear. They moved southeastward as far as Fiji, and then struck out into the unknown in their big double canoes.

By 1000 B.C., Polynesians had settled in Samoa and Tonga, fertile island groups where the living was good; but still there were pioneers who sailed on to the east.

Sailing canoe
of Tahiti, 1792.

Defeat in battle, a family quarrel, the banishment of a man for evildoing, or simply the spirit of adventure—all these were good reasons to leave one's home village and look for a better life beyond the horizon. Some of the Polynesian sailors were storm-driven and made their landfalls by accident. Others arrived on new islands prepared to settle down, bringing with them live pigs, chickens, and dogs and a stock of taro roots and coconuts.

Canoes of Tonga,
early 19th century.

An island, once found, could be found again by the Polynesian navigators. At night they set a course by chosen stars. By day they watched for the pillars of cloud that rise above the crests of high volcanic islands, or the dim green reflection on a cloudy sky, which marks the presence of a low atoll, a necklace of islets around a shallow green lagoon. When evening came, the flight of homing seabirds would often lead the navigator to a safe landing on an island beach.

By 200 B.C., the Polynesians had reached Tahiti and the Marquesas, and from these island groups, adventurers sailed on to distant Easter Island, north across the open sea to Hawaii, and southwestward to New Zealand.

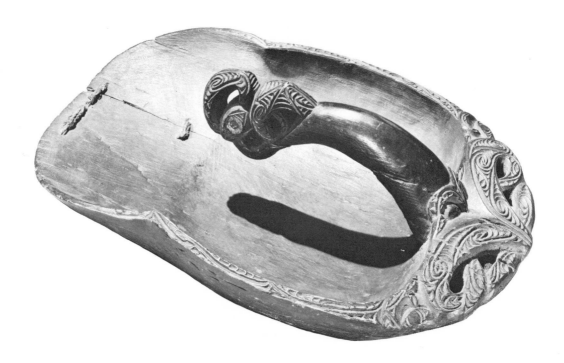

Wooden canoe bailer.
Maori, New Zealand.

The heroic Polynesian navigators and the canoes they sailed in are still remembered today in song, dance, and story on the islands where they settled. Even the names of the canoes and the tales of their building are not forgotten.

The making of a canoe, from the cutting of wood in the forest to the launching in the sea, was a holy task. Canoe builders prayed and fasted and asked the blessing of the gods on their work. Their principal tool was the adze, which had a finely ground blade of stone or shell. To the Polynesian craftsman, the adze itself was sacred, filled with its own mysterious power. In Tahiti, before work began on a new canoe, the adzes of the craftsmen were "put to sleep" overnight in a temple and ceremonially washed in the sea in the morning.

Working adze with stone blade. Tahiti.

The canoe builder knew what wood to choose for making the hull and outrigger of his vessel or the twin hulls of a double canoe. Usually a large tree was hollowed out to make a shallow dugout, and the sides of the hull were then built up with planks, hewn with the adze.

Carver using an adze.
Palau, Caroline Islands.

Finding enough wood was no problem on high islands where the mountainsides rising from the shore were thickly forested, but on coral atolls, especially in 'Micronesia, wood was scarce. The hulls of Micronesian canoes were often built of many small pieces fitted together, and the art of wood carving, so rich and elaborate in Polynesia, was severely simple. Yet a wooden box for fishing tackle, a necessity aboard a Micronesian canoe, could be shaped into a fine form. The box below is even inlaid with shell, one of the few materials plentiful in the Gilbert Islands, where this box was made. The Gilbertese carvers had no stone for their adze blades and had to make them from the shell of the giant clam.

Wooden tackle box.
Gilbert Islands.

Shells, highly prized by the sea people, were also used for decorating canoes. In Melanesia, the great war canoes of the western Solomon Islands were inlaid with shell which showed up brilliantly white against the blackened wood-work of the long, lean hulls. The high prows were bordered with large white cowries, and at the waterline a wood-carved figure was attached, representing the guardian spirit of the canoe. This, too, was often inlaid with shell.

These *tomoko* canoes, built to carry warriors on head-hunting raids, had no outriggers, and their narrow hulls were made entirely of planks, with curved ribs inside for extra strength. Ribs and planks were lashed together with strong cord. The builders of *tomoko* used lengths of *loya* vine for lashing; most of the sea people used sennit, the cord made from the outer fibers of coconut husks.

Interior of a plank-built canoe.
Ulawa, Solomon Islands.

Fibers from other island plants were spun into thread and string, but coconut fiber was, and still is, by far the most important. Sennit bound together the beams of houses, as well as the planks and outriggers of canoes and the blades and handles of the craftsmen's tools.

The making of sennit was traditionally the work of older men. Even today, a dignified Polynesian chief, who leaves manual labor to the young men of his household, will sit for hours and roll out the twisted cords of sennit on his bare thigh.

Tomoko *canoe and canoe house.*
New Georgia, Solomon Islands.

13

When the planks of a canoe had been fitted together, the sennit was threaded through small holes along the edges and pulled tight. While they worked on the sennit lashings, the canoe builders of Tahiti would sing to Tane, the god of the wood-carvers:

> What have I, O Tane,
> O Tane, god of beauty?
>   'Tis sennit!
> 'Tis sennit of the host of heaven,
> 'Tis sennit for thee, O Tane!
> Thread it from inside, it comes outside.
> Thread it from outside, it comes inside.
> Tie it fully, tie it fast.
> This is the fashion of thy sennit,
>   O Tane,
> To hold thy canoe,
> That she may go over long waves,
> And over short waves;
> To the near horizon,
> Even to the far-off horizon.
> This sennit of thine, O Tane,
> Let it hold, let it hold!

Roofbeams of a house
bound together with sennit.
Gilbert Islands.

Sennit also provided the strong cordage for rigging, while sails were made from the leaves of the *pandanus*, a hardy tree that flourished even on the most barren atolls. The long, thin leaves were dried and split and woven into mats by the women's skillful fingers. Strips of pandanus matting, sewn together, made strong sails to harness the power of the wind and send the canoes, like birds, across the sea.

Lashing together
the planks of a canoe.
Gilbert Islands.

Long after the islands were settled and the great migrations were over, canoes still sailed the ocean. The white men who came to explore the Pacific in the seventeenth and eighteenth centuries marveled at the speed and perform-ance of the island craft.

But canoes were far more than seaworthy vessels, their design perfected by the experi-ence of generations of seamen. Canoes were an expression of spiritual things, the beliefs that governed the lives of the island peoples. The carved prows, spirit images, shell inlay, and streaming feather plumes were symbols of the people's faith in the gods and of their feeling of kinship with the living creatures that shared their island world.

Canoes were works of art, created by artists who were highly respected. Wherever canoes were made and used for fishing, trading, raid-ing, or far-sea voyaging, there we shall look for the rich art heritage of the people of the sea.

Above: Masthead of Fijian ndrua.
Opposite: Ndrua—*great double canoe of Fiji.*

Today the great canoes are gone. Travelers go by ship between the islands or take the planes that fly high over the ocean, casting their moving shadows on the empty blue water. The pattern of islands, reefs, and brilliant green lagoons is the same that the old seamen knew, but the lifeways of the islanders have changed.

The ancient unity of man and nature was shattered by the coming of the white men. The newcomers brought iron to the Stone Age peoples of the Pacific, who quickly saw its benefits; but along with the white men's wonderful goods came the scourge of disease. Whole villages were wiped out by sickness, from which there was no escape. The old gods were powerless to help the people who had served them so faithfully. Many of the islanders accepted the new faith and new learning offered to them by Western missionaries. Old arts and the customs and beliefs that had nourished them were swept away, often by the islanders themselves.

Yet underneath the surface changes, ancient traditions are still woven into the stuff of life. On small islands and atolls, remote from the shipping lanes, the sea is still a road to adventure. Here the village canoe house down by the shore, where boats are built and repaired, is the center of art and craft, the place for discussions and judgments, for the planning of a voyage and the teaching of navigation.

The people of the sea, especially the women, have never lost their gift for making beautiful things from simple materials. Today old skills are being revived and new forms of art created. The islanders' love of music and dance, reaching far back into the past, is still as strong as ever, and any occasion for celebration can become a festival of dancing.

Then Western clothes are discarded, and the ancient arts of dress and decoration come alive again, arts to be seen in action, adorning the bodies of the dancers and moving to the stamp of feet and the joyful music of song.

Opposite: Trading canoe with traditional matting sails.
Siassi Islands, Papua New Guinea.

2

Feathers, Fibers, and Leaves

Yapese dancers, whirling in the swift rhythms of a festival dance, wear costumes of feathers, flowers, and fresh coconut fronds. The dance skirts that swing about their hips are of shining white hibiscus fiber dyed in bright colors. Their faces are painted, and their bodies gleam with coconut oil.

Village dancers
performing a Mit-Mit.
Yap, Caroline Islands.

On the island of Yap, at the western edge of Micronesia, old traditions are strong, and the people are well known for their skill in dancing. Some of their dances and songs come from the outer islands, dotted over the sea to the east, scraps of land that were dominated by Yap in the days before the white men came. The swift canoes of the islanders brought regular tribute to Gagil, the Yapese town that held power over the outer islands. The people offered dances and songs along with their pandanus matting, coconut cord, and textiles finely woven on the loom.

Yapese dancers
dressed for the Mit-Mit.

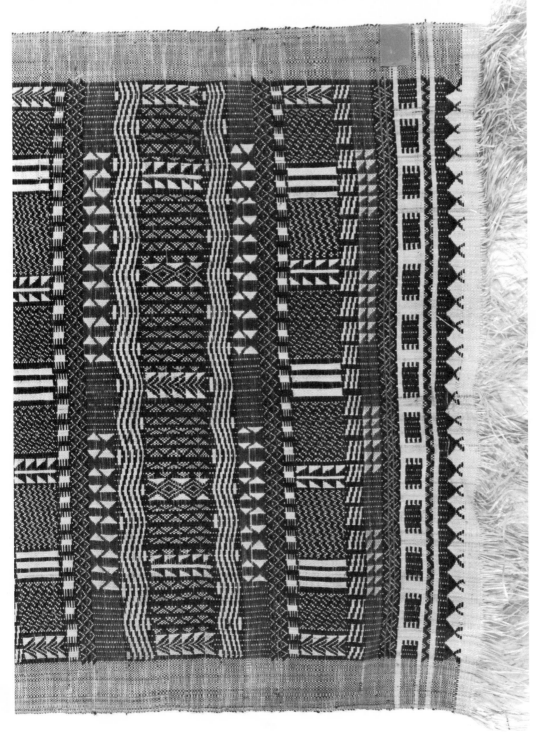

One end of a woven lavalava—
a woman's wraparound skirt.
Fais, Caroline Islands.

Variations of the Yapese dance costume can be seen far and wide among the sea peoples. Even the men of Fiji, leaping and lunging in the war dances of old, are decked in leaves and garlands and carry woven dance fans in their hands.

Fijian dancers
performing a meke.

24

But the most spectacular dance costumes are to be found along the shores of New Guinea and on some of the islands of Melanesia. There the faces and bodies of dancers may be hidden by masks, transforming them into fantastic beings from another world.

At a village on the north coast of New Guinea, gigantic masks made of feathers appear mysteriously once a year. Stalking through the village, awesome and magnificent, they represent the gods of the people. Yet these towering creations last only for the time of the festival. As part of the ceremony, the masks must be dismantled. The great rattan frames on which the feathers are mounted are destroyed, but the precious feathers are saved.

*Feather masks. Awar,
Papua New Guinea.*

25

26

Feathers have always had a deep significance for the sea people. The islands are poor in four-footed animals, but birds are plentiful. Seabirds are guides for the navigator seeking a landfall and for the fisherman on the lookout for schooling fish. In the past, birds were closely linked with the gods, and their bodies could serve as carriers for the spirits of the dead.

Although feathers of all colors were made into headdresses and costumes, red feathers have always been the most highly prized, worn by chiefs and even used as money.

The feathered scepter, called a *kahili*, was the sacred symbol of royalty in Hawaii. The largest *kahili*, for display on great occasions, would be named after a royal ancestor, and its handle might be made from the bone of a noble enemy killed in battle. The feathers were removed from the *kahili* after use and carefully stored away.

Opposite: Hawaiian in a feathered helmet and cloak, 1784. Above: Kahili—*feathered scepter. Hawaii.*

The feather cloaks and helmets of Hawaii, worn only by chiefs, were the work of special craftsmen. The cloaks ranged in size from short capes to flowing mantles that swept the ground. Thousands of feathers were fastened to a strong netting of *olona* fiber to make a cloak. At first only the red feathers of *'i'iwi* birds were used. Later these were mixed with the rare yellow plumage of the *'o'o* and arranged in geometric designs. Both birds were tiny honey eaters, and feather hunters went to the forest to trap them at the season of molting. The yellow feathers could be plucked and the birds released to grow new ones, but the red birds were killed and skinned.

The Maori of New Zealand, thousands of miles to the south, also made feather cloaks for people of high rank. The one above is covered with pigeon feathers, dark green and white, with a border of the brown plumage of the flightless kiwi. Whole cloaks of kiwi feathers look almost as though they are made of fur.

Opposite: Feather cloak. Hawaii.
Above: Cloak of pigeon feathers.
Maori, New Zealand, 1910.

29

Such warm clothing was more than a sign of prestige for the Maori; it was a necessity in the cold climate of the land where they settled. The Maori pioneers had discovered a country very different from the warm islands of eastern Polynesia that had been their home. It was too cold for most of the familiar tropical trees and plants, but the soil was fertile for farming, and the forests offered limitless wood for the carver and the builders of houses and canoes.

Maori council house
with people in traditional
and European dress.

The land promised the people a good life, with time to spare from farming, fishing, and hunting to work with their hands. Old arts and skills were developed and the new art of weaving textiles was born.

The fiber of the flax plant, which the Maori used for making fishing nets, could be woven into warm cloth; but perfecting the technique took years of trial and effort. With no knowledge of looms, the Maori women used a finger-weaving method. Warp threads were hung on a wooden frame, and the work began at the top as the horizontal weft threads were twined around the warps. Ample, full-length cloaks were made in this way, and flax weaving also served as a base for the chiefs' cloaks of feathers. As the weavers' skill increased, they made war cloaks with fabric so dense that it would repel the thrust of a spear.

Flax cloak. Maori, New Zealand.

31

Cloaks were often decorated with black tags of cord knotted into the weaving, but the finer ones had broad patterned borders of tightly woven cloth called *taniko*. The threads used for *taniko* were dyed brownish red, black and sometimes yellow—colors that combined beautifully with the golden tone of a silky flaxen cloak.

Taniko designs varied from one tribal group to another, but all were strictly geometric and angular, limited by the rigid and difficult technique. The weavers' patterns are in sharp contrast to the curves, spirals, and scrolls that are typical of other Maori arts.

Opposite: Part of the taniko *border of a flax cloak. Maori. Above: Typical Maori designs engraved on a gourd vessel.*

After the European settlement of New Zealand, the Maori weavers enriched their *taniko* with colored wools bought from white traders. Some splendid cloaks were made in the nineteenth century. This one is unusual in being striped with *taniko* from top to bottom.

Taniko weaving, a living art among the Maori people today, is a testimony to the skill and imagination of their ancestors in adapting to life in a strange land and creating new arts from the materials they found there.

Everywhere, the sea peoples had to make the best use they could of the resources of their islands. The Maori found a large, rich land that gave them all they needed, but many of the sea peoples were not as fortunate. The Gilbert Islanders, as we have seen, had few materials to work with. Like the Maori, the Gilbertese were often embroiled in wars. They fought with swords, spears, and daggers edged with sharks' teeth—razor-sharp. Without protective clothing in battle, too many warriors would have been killed.

Cloak of woven flax and
taniko. *Maori, about 1850.*

35

The coconut tree, plentiful on the Gilbert Islands, provided the material for the unique Gilbertese armor, woven of tough coconut cord. The armor above is reinforced with a breastplate of sharkskin. A complete suit included sleeves, leggings, and a helmet, which might be covered with the skin of a blowfish, bristling with spines.

Body armor of sennit and sharkskin. Gilbert Islands.

The Gilbert Islanders were, and still are, skilled weavers of pandanus mats and baskets, but the loom-weaving art of Micronesia has never spread to their islands. The early settlers of the Small Islands brought from their old homes in Indonesia their knowledge of weaving with the backstrap loom. Woven textiles, as we have seen, were part of the tribute brought to Yap from the outer islands. And in the past, the Yapese themselves were weavers. This weaving art was restricted to the Carolines, the central island chain that stretches from Yap in the west to the high islands of Kosrae and Ponape in the east.

According to old tradition, the Carolines were linked together in a seafaring empire, of which Yap and its small dependents were only a part. The empire lasted until the sixteenth century, and its rulers were famous navigators. How strong a hold they had over the many scattered islands is hard to tell, but some of the rulers must have been men of wealth and power. The ruins of ancient stone palaces still stand on Kosrae and Ponape, and on these two islands the art of the weavers reached its peak.

Weaver with backstrap loom.
Ulithi, Caroline Islands.

Long after the coming of the first white men, the weavers of Kosrae and Ponape continued to produce their masterpieces, the long sashes worn by nobles. These beautiful belts were woven of fine threads of banana fiber, naturally golden in color or dyed red. In the chief's belt opposite, the two colors of fiber are combined with threads of wool in red, yellow, and blue, bought from the white men. The principal patterns of these belts were not in the weft but in the warp threads, set up on the loom before the weaving began. Warps of different colors were arranged in stripes, and short sections of varying color were knotted into the warp threads to produce more intricate patterns. There were sometimes more than eighty warps to the inch.

The chief's belt below, from Ponape, also includes red wool, as well as banana fiber. Its border is of tiny disks of white shell, and imported glass beads of red, yellow, black, and white have been woven into the design.

Woven sash. Ponape, Caroline Islands.

38

The making of these belts is an art of the past, but women's skirts are still woven on the outer islands of the old Yapese empire. These *lavalavas* are strips of material to be worn wrapped tightly around the hips and reaching from waist to knee. The weavers use banana fiber or threads of the same creamy white hibiscus fiber that is made into dancing skirts by the women of Yap. Dyed hibiscus and colored imported cotton are combined in rich woven designs, some of them passed down without change through generations of weavers. (See page 23.)

Woven sash. Kosrae,
Caroline Islands.

In the Marshall Islands, east of the Carolines, traditional clothing was made of woven pandanus matting, as thin and supple as cloth and decorated with borders of colored weaving. The women of the Marshalls were also good weavers of fans, a common craft of the people of the sea. In the islands of eastern Polynesia, a well-made fan in the hand of a chief was a symbol of high social position.

The fine pandanus mat was also important among the Polynesians, not as an item of dress but as a form of wealth. In Samoa today, fine mats are presented to the most honored people on ceremonial occasions and treasured in families as heirlooms.

For their clothing, the people of tropical Polynesia depended chiefly on *tapa*, cloth made from the bark of the paper mulberry tree. The decoration of tapa was one of the two principal graphic arts of the sea people. The other was the honored art of *tatu*, the adornment of the human skin with never-fading designs for a lifetime's admiration and delight.

Corner of a woven mat.
Marshall Islands.

40

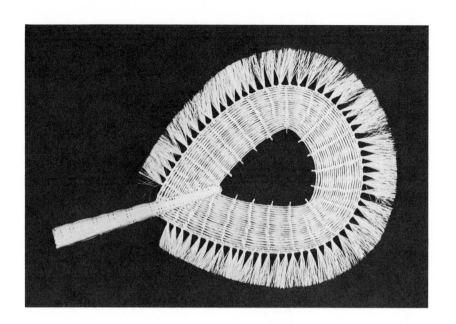

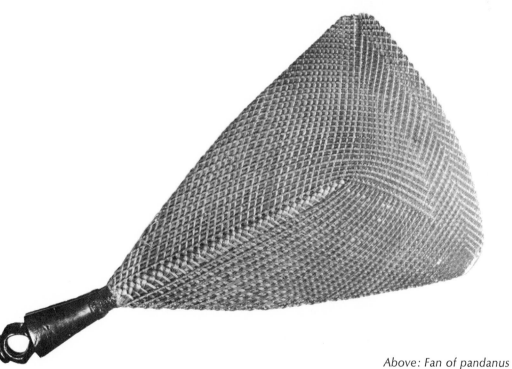

Above: Fan of pandanus fiber with turtle shell center. Marshall Islands. Below: Fan woven of coconut leaflets. Tahiti.

3

Tapa
and
Tatu

Tapa was not only a beautiful dress material for the people of tropical islands. It also played an important role in religious rites and ceremonial gift giving, and was even used for making masks.

Imported cotton cloth, replacing tapa for everyday dress, has killed the craft of the tapa maker in many parts of Polynesia, but in Tonga and Samoa, bark cloth is still produced for home use and for sale. On these islands, and in Fiji to the west, the *thump-thump* of the bark beater echoes through the villages, and the making of fine bark cloth is a lively art.

The tapa makers are women, and everywhere they follow similar methods of preparing the cloth. The best tapa is made from mulberry bark, though the bark of breadfruit and fig trees is also used. Small trees are felled, the bark is peeled off in long strips, and the outer covering scraped away from the white inner fiber. The strips of fiber are dried and then soaked to soften them for beating. Laid across a smooth log anvil, each strip gradually grows thinner and wider under the steady thumping blows of the wooden beater. A number of strips are felted together by more beating until the piece of tapa is the right size and thickness, a fine white cloth ready to be decorated with homemade dyes.

Opposite: Painted tapa of
Polynesia. Austral Islands.
Above: Tapa mask. Papuan Gulf.

43

The most usual colors for tapa today are shades of brown, made from the bark of trees; black, from the soot of burned candlenuts; and red, from red clay. Purple, green, blue, and many other colors were used in the past, especially in Hawaii.

Presentation tapa for
a ceremonial occasion.
Lau Islands, Fiji.

Samoan women decorate their tapa by painting, as their ancestors did, but they begin by making a rubbing. The plain cloth is laid over a wooden board like a large relief-printing block, and the surface is rubbed with red pigment. The relief pattern of the block comes through on the cloth, and then the design is accented by painting over it in dark brown.

The beautiful Tongan tapa is decorated by the same method of rubbing and painting. Instead of the wooden board, the Tongans use a design tablet called a *kupesi*, which is made from pandanus leaves with the thin ribs of coconut fronds stitched on, making a raised linear pattern.

Designs painted on tapa. Samoa.

Some *kupesi* are very small with a single motif that can be repeated. The large one above comes from Fiji, where the tapa makers of the Lau Islands, not far from Tonga by canoe, often use Tongan techniques and patterns. The great Fijian tapa on page 44, made for presentation at a ceremony, is decorated in the Tongan way. The handsome piece opposite shows typical Fijian designs combined with rubbings from a *kupesi* for the background. Stencils, cut from banana leaves, were used to create the repeating patterns in black and reddish brown that stand out boldly on the pure white tapa.

Left: Kupesi—*design tablet for*
making patterns on tapa. Fiji.
Right: Detail of tapa design. Tonga.

An equally dramatic contrast of black and white appears in the designs on the old bark cloth masks of the Papuan Gulf, like the one on page 43. Here the white tapa was stretched on a frame, and cutout designs in painted tapa were fastened on. These masks were made by men, working in secret in the men's meetinghouse of their village. Scores of masks were needed for the performance of a ceremony that would bring blessing and good fortune to the people.

Decorated tapa. Kabara, Lau Islands, Fiji.

A company of mighty spirit masks, also made of painted tapa, were the chief actors in the drama. Their wearers, carrying long vase-shaped drums to make rhythm for the dance, were transformed into spirits of the forest and sea, kindly beings whose visits to the village were rare and long expected. When the spirits departed, after nearly a month of ceremonies, the tall sacred masks were returned to the men's house and burned.

Large tapa masks.
Papuan Gulf.

While there was no masking tradition in Polynesia, many Polynesian people wore what amounted to a permanent mask—a mask of tatu. Among the Maori, the tatu artist showed his greatest skill in the adornment of the face. Etched deep into the skin were the same elaborate curves and scrolls that the Maori carved in wood. Women's facial tatu, restricted to the mouth and chin, was in a similar style. The pattern for each person, individually designed, was a mark of beauty and a sign of courage, for the pain of its making was hard to bear. The Maori said that men learned about tatu from the spirits of the underworld. The Maori tatu artist ranked as a priest, wise in the rituals of his sacred art.

Maori with facial tatu. New Zealand.

49

The glories of tatu are only a memory in most of the Polynesian islands today, for the art was outlawed in the nineteenth century, when the people became Christians. Before that time, the finest Polynesian tatu was to be seen in the Marquesas. People there wore few clothes, and their bodies were covered with a living fabric of fantastic design. A complete tatu took years to finish, beginning when a girl was ten or twelve and a boy a few years older. The same tatu artist had to carry through the work to the end. To help his client in the choice of designs, he might display a wooden arm or leg carved with an elegant arrangement of patterns. The chosen designs, once they were etched on the skin, would come alive with every movement of the body.

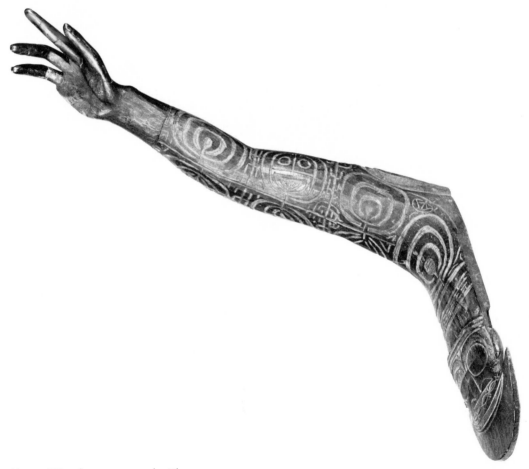

Above: Wooden arm carved with tatu designs. Marquesas Islands. Opposite: A man of the Marquesas with tatu, early 19th century.

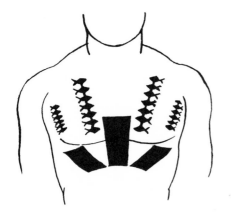

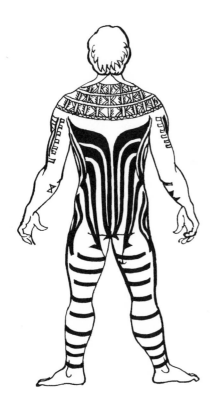

Above: Man's chest tatu.
Bellona, Solomon Islands.
Below: Man's body tatu.
Sonsorol, Caroline Islands.

Tatu is still a respected art on the island of Bellona, a small outpost of Polynesian people in the Solomon Islands. A shoal of fish is a favorite pattern to wear on the chest. For chiefs there is a sacred chest tatu, which a young chief must prove himself worthy to receive. People say this pattern was a gift from the high god of Bellona, and in ancient times it served as a magic breastplate to protect the chief in battle.

The people of Micronesia were lavishly adorned with tatu, and they also believed that the art was a gift from the gods. An old story of the Caroline Islands tells how the god Wolfat came down from heaven one night with beautiful tatu all over his body. He was so much admired by the island women that the men began to paint their skins in imitation of the god's tatu, and he kindly revealed to them the secrets of the art.

He showed them how to carve a tool like a tiny comb from the wing bone of a frigate bird, and how to make black ink from the soot of burning breadfruit gum mixed with water in a coconut shell. Then he taught them how the designs were painted on the body and made indelible by piercing the skin with the tool, which was lightly tapped with a small hammer.

The delicate tools of the artist and the process of making pricked tatu varied little among the island peoples. In Polynesia, only the Maori had their own alternative technique, which resulted in a deeply carved effect, the pride of Maori warriors.

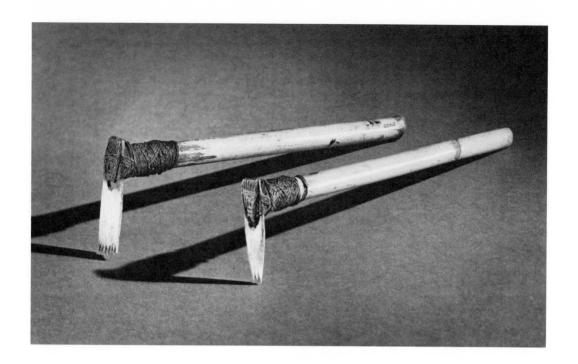

Like the decoration of tapa, tatu was an art to be enjoyed for its own sake, a matter of personal taste rather than stern necessity. Yet the artistry of the island peoples was expressed in everything they made, even the tools of their work.

The precision instruments of the tatu artist are small masterpieces of craftsmanship, made from the commonest materials—wood, fiber, and sharpened bone.

The bones of birds and fish, along with the shells of creatures of the sea, could be found in plenty on almost all the islands and took the place of metal for the island people. But bone and shell were not only made into blades for cutting tools. They also provided materials for a wealth of other crafts, from the making of fishhooks to the finest jewelry.

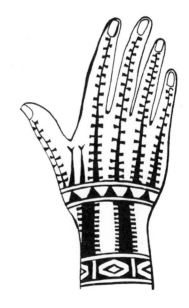

Above: Tatu artist's tools, Fiji.
Below: Woman's hand tatu.
Ponape, Caroline Islands.

53

4

Bone and Shell

A fishhook for catching bonito was worthy to become an heirloom, passed down in the family of the master fisherman. Old stories tell of hooks with magic power, promising their owners a good catch. Bonito were caught by trolling from the stern of a canoe, and skill, as well as magic, was needed by the fisherman.

The making of the bonito hook, with point and shank carved separately and lashed together, was an art in itself, widespread among the people of the sea. The largest trolling hooks, like the two at the left, were made in Tonga. There the shanks were carved of whalebone and faced with shell, the points cut from the shell of the sea turtle.

The hook at the right, from Micronesia, also has a bone shank and turtle shell point; but most hooks had shanks of pearl shell, varying in color from white to gold or gray.

Opposite: Large trolling hooks. Tonga.
Above: Turtle shell hook. Ponape, Caroline Islands.
Right: Fishhook of bone and shell. Tobi, Caroline Islands.

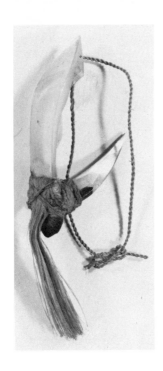

Left: Shell fishhooks.
(top) Marshall Islands.
(bottom) Caroline Islands.
Right: Three shell
pendants. Solomon Islands.

According to the lore of the fishermen, the shape and color of the bonito hook are important in attracting the fish. Men of the western Solomons say that a fisherman needs six hooks of different colors. He chooses which to use by noting the color of the small fry on which the bonito are feeding. Great black frigate birds also gather to prey on the small fish and serve the fisherman as guides, leading him to the bonito.

The frigate bird and school of fish, familiar in the lives of the people, are common themes in Solomon Islands art. We see them in the decoration of clamshell pendants, a favorite form of jewelry. On the crescent-shaped pendant at the left, the soaring frigate bird appears alone, cut out of a thin slice of turtle shell. The small round pendant from the Santa Cruz Islands, home of famous navigators, has the bird and fish designs combined.

Men dressed for a dance
wearing shell pendants.
Santa Cruz Islands.

Round shell ornaments, overlaid with intricate turtle shell open-work, can also be found far eastward across the Pacific, in the Marquesas. Their patterns recall the rich designs of Marquesan tatu. The people of those islands delighted in jewelry. Women wore little earplugs, made from the bones of their ancestors and often carved in the form of tiny human figures. The round shell plaques were mounted on woven headbands and proudly worn by warriors.

Turtle shell, so delicately cut to make these ornaments, was also carved into graceful fishhooks, like the one on page 55.

Ornaments from the Marquesas.
Above: Bone ear ornaments.
Below: Headband with shell disk.

Among the people of the Torres Strait, living on a group of small islands between New Guinea and Australia, turtle shell fish-hooks were a necessary part of the bride-price when a girl got married, and the bride herself would wear an engraved shell pendant shaped like a hook.

The men of the Torres Strait, bold seafarers, turtle hunters, and fishermen, were unrivaled in their artistic use of turtle shell. By steaming the shell to make it soft and pliable, and carefully fitting many pieces together, they created a unique form of art—the turtle shell mask.

Lively fish-shaped masks, trimmed with the plumes of the cassowary, danced in a ritual to increase the harvest of fish from the sea, the food that gave life to the people.

Fish-shaped mask made of turtle shell. Torres Strait.

On the island of Mer, in the eastern Torres Strait, a dancer wearing a human mask of turtle shell would appear at the time of death and play the part of the dead person in a funeral pantomime.

In contrast to this realistic mask, complete with hair and beard, is the majestic costume opposite, made for a funeral in Tahiti. This was the customary dress of the priest or the principal mourner in the ceremonies following the death of a Tahitian chief. Plates of pearl shell, like bright armor, hide the face of the wearer. The headdress is crowned with seabird plumes, and a black feather cloak forms the background for the shimmering garment of narrow strips of shell that hangs across the body.

The beauty of polished pearl shell is also displayed in the ceremonial headdress of a *taupou*, the daughter of a Samoan chief. A tall headdress like the one on page 62, with shells, feathers, and bushy wig, is still the proper adornment for the village *taupou* when she performs her traditional role, preparing the drink of kava for an assembly of chiefs. (See page 87.)

Opposite: Mourning costume. Tahiti.
Above: Turtle shell mask for funeral
ceremonies. Torres Strait.

Left: Shell money. Solomon Islands.
Right: Headdress of the taupou for
the kava ceremony. Samoa.

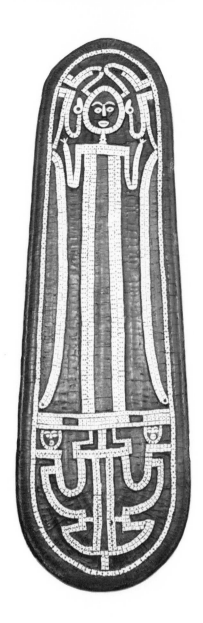

Shell, in all its variety, was a versatile material for the artist. Light and delicate in the decoration of a headdress, shell could also be heavy and hard as stone. In the western Solomons, the fossilized shell of the giant clam was used for making carved memorial tablets for the dead. These marked the shrines where the skulls of warriors were preserved and where people paid homage to their ancestors, leaving offerings of clamshell money—white rings, smooth as marble.

The shell money and memorials were made by the slow and patient techniques of the stone carver. The Stone Age people of the sea knew well how to work with stone. Wherever stone could be found, it was put to many uses by the carver and builder.

Left: Clamshell memorial carving
for a grave. Solomon Islands.
Right: Ceremonial shield of wickerwork
and shell. Solomon Islands.

63

5

Stone for the Carver and Builder

The village pathways of Yap, often paved with stone, are lined with huge moon-shaped pieces of stone money. The biggest pieces, old and moss-grown, lean against the ancient stone platforms of the houses and proclaim the wealth of the village to all who pass by. Smaller pieces of money change hands to buy a pig or a tract of land, or to pay the dancers at a village festival.

The Yapese art of carving stone money would have been impossible without their skill in seamanship. The money was carved of limestone, quarried in the islands of Palau, 250 miles to the south. A legendary Yapese navigator, Anagumang, discovered the white Palauan stone and decreed that the money should be round in shape, like the full moon. The work of quarrying the stones and bringing them home to Yap by canoe was hard and dangerous, and many stones were named after men who had died on the journey. The largest money was made late in the nineteenth century and transported in the ships of white men, principally those of the famous trader, Captain O'Keefe.

On the island of Ponape, at the far eastern end of the long Caroline chain, stone was used in a different way. Here, the majestic ruins of Nan Matol, the stone-built city of the rulers of Ponape, tower above the green shallows of the coastal lagoon. The builders constructed fifty artificial islands on the reef, so that the city's streets are canals, traversed by canoe. The high walls —sometimes 40 feet high—are built of huge "logs" of basalt from the main island of Ponape, natural formations of rock, untrimmed by the builders.

Opposite: Stone money.
Yap, Caroline Islands.

An ancient legend says that the stone city was founded by two magicians, and at their summons the stones flew into place by themselves. Nan Matol was later seized by men from the island of Kosrae, where there are ruins of another palace-city built of stone. The age of Nan Matol is still unknown, and an air of mystery hangs over the silent courtyards. Here we see no decoration, no carving, only the massive piling up of uncut stone. The men of Ponape and Kosrae were mighty builders, but carving in stone was not a strong tradition in Micronesia. We must turn to the many islands of Polynesia to find stone sculpture in the round.

The most famous sculptures of the Pacific were carved of stone by the people of Rapa Nui. This lonely fragment of land that white men call Easter Island was settled by Polynesian pioneers from the Marquesas about A.D. 400. They found themselves on an island of stone. Wood for the carver was scarce and small in size. Even shells were lacking in the cold and stormy seas. Carvers of stone became the most highly respected of the island's artists.

Above: Ruins of Nan Matol. Ponape,
Caroline Islands.
Opposite: Stone images. Easter Island.

Noble families vied with each other in erecting monuments of stone. Along the rocky shore they built *ahu*—stone platforms—on which they placed enormous statues as memorials to their honored dead. The giant figures were carved from soft rock in the crater of an extinct volcano and then hauled down to the sea. Some still lie unfinished in the quarry, while others stand on the bare slopes of the volcano, as though they had suddenly stopped on the long march to the *ahu*.

*Stone images on the slopes
of Rano Raraku, Easter Island.*

The statues that eventually reached the shore were lined up on the platforms with their backs to the water, and the heads were crowned with red stone "topknots," cut from a quarry of red rock. When war broke out between the island clans in the seventeenth and eighteenth centuries, all the statues on the *ahu* were thrown down and shattered.

Rock carving of birdman.
Orongo, Easter Island.

69

This finely carved figure, smaller than the *ahu* statues, survived intact and was found in the village of Orongo, where the islanders gathered for the yearly festival of the Birdman. (See page 113.) The boulders at Orongo are covered with petroglyphs. Deeply cut rock pictures show bird-headed men and the staring face of Make Make, protector of seabirds and chief god of the Easter Island people. It was Make Make, the creator, whose power brought new life each spring to the fishing grounds and the stony land, as well as to the nesting birds. In other parts of Polynesia, where Make Make was unknown, the power of creation was embodied in the *tiki*, a human figure that could represent either the creator who made the first man or the first man himself. Tiki could be large or small. We have seen these figures in miniature, carved on bone earplugs from the Marquesas.

Stone image from Orongo, Easter Island.

Small stone-carved tiki were worn as pendants by the Marquesans and also by the Maori. The figure above, with head tilted on one side and eyes inlaid with shell, is typical of many made by Maori artists. They were carved of green nephrite, a stone so hard that it could only be worked by patient rubbing with water, sand, and sandstone. Tiki like this one were passed down in Maori families and were supposed to insure that their wearers would have many children.

Stone tiki in the form of a pendant. Maori.

The small tiki of the Marquesas, carved of rather rough basaltic rock, were sometimes made in pairs, joined back to back. The Marquesans were great builders and carvers, and their mountainous green islands provided them with plenty of stone.

Small double tiki
carved of stone.
Marquesas Islands.

In the sixteenth and seventeenth centuries, the time of the *ahu* and giant statues of Easter Island, the Marquesans were erecting *marae* in the tropical forest—vast temple platforms in which some of the building stones were 8 feet high. Here, in wooden god-houses, they set up stone images of the gods like the weather-worn tiki above, one of the few still standing in its ancient place.

The ancestors of these Marquesan builders and carvers were seafarers from Tonga and Samoa, sailing eastward in their canoes 2,000 years ago. One of the Polynesian crafts and skills that they brought with them was the women's art of making pottery. Although the potters found clay to work with in the newly discovered islands, their art died out and was forgotten. Only the sherds of ancient pots remain.

Traditional pottery making, once an important part of life, is unknown today among the Polynesian people; but among the Fijians on the border of Polynesia, it is still a living art.

Large stone tiki still in its original place. Marquesas Islands.

6

Clay for the Potter

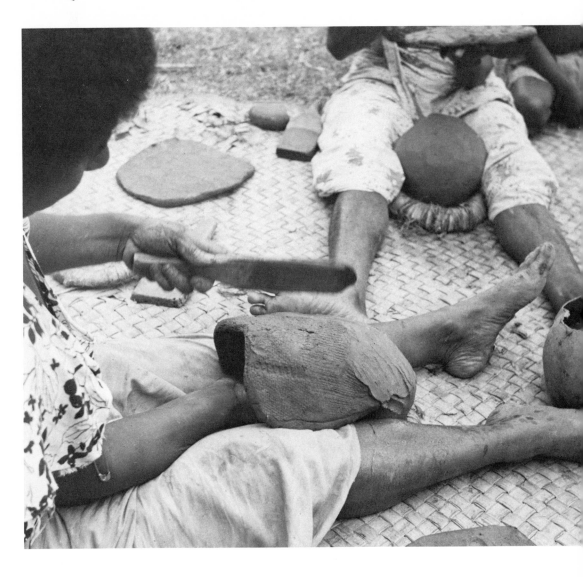

The broad green valley of the Sigatoka River has been a center of Fijian pottery making for hundreds of years. Coming down from the mountains of the interior, the big river meets the sea on the sandy southern coast of Viti Levu, the main island of the Fijian group.

In the river valley the women of the pottery villages dig clay from the earth and mix it with fine sand, to prepare it for their work. Most of the pots they make are *kuro*, large plain vessels for cooking over an open fire. The principal tools of the potters are wooden paddles and smooth round river pebbles that they use as anvils. The paddle and anvil are the tools of village potters in other parts of the world, from India to Peru, but no one builds a pot in the same way as the women of the Sigatoka Valley.

The shaping of the pot begins with thick slabs of clay, joined together to make a rough cylindrical form. The paddle in the left hand beats the soft clay over the anvil stone, held inside the pot.

Opposite: Fijian potter begins
shaping the first cylindrical form.
Above: Three stages in making a pot.

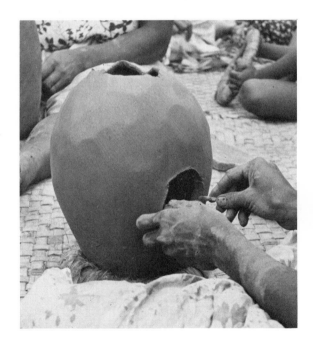

Above: The rough form of the pot is shaped with paddle and anvil. Below: Cutting the hole in the wall of the pot.

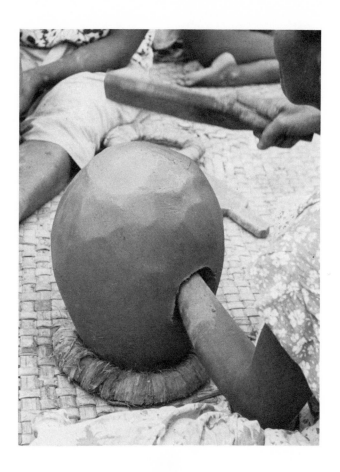

Then the cylinder is placed on a supporting stand, a circlet of twisted leaves; and swift tapping of paddle on clay gradually thins out and shapes the walls to a swelling curve. Next a fist-sized hole is cut in the body of the pot with a bamboo knife. The thick piece of clay taken out is used to close the open top, and the newly cut hole allows the hand holding the anvil to work inside the pot.

When this stage is complete, the egg-shaped clay form is left to dry until it is hard enough to be turned upside down without losing its shape. What had been the top now becomes a thick, sturdy base. A round hole is opened in the new top to make the mouth of the pot, and the cutout circle of clay is smoothed over the hole in the side. Now the body of the vessel is finished.

Closing the top of the pot and beating it smooth.

Walking around the pot, the woman shapes the rim and adds more clay to form the flared lip. Then she sets the pot aside to dry for several days before she fires it in an open fire.

No decoration is added to village cooking pots, but vessels made for sale to outsiders are rubbed over with resin while they are hot from the firing. This leaves a coat of shiny varnish that brings out the red-orange color of the clay and the black smoky marks of the fire.

In the past, Fijian pottery was more ornate and varied in shape, especially the work of the Rewa River potters on the eastern side of Viti Levu. This handsome Rewa water jar was used in a Fijian temple about 100 years ago, before the people became Christian.

Opposite: Finishing Fijian cooking pot; shaping the lip. Above: Pottery water jar. Fiji, early 19th century.

Among the ancient forms of Fijian pots is the peculiar type of water vessel shaped like a bunch of fruit, still made by Rewa River potters for sale to visitors. Besides the *kuro*, wide bowls called *dari* are traditional in the Sigatoka Valley. The woman opposite is making one with paddle and anvil, and she will decorate it around the rim in the old way, by pressing patterns into the damp clay with the serrated edge of a shell.

The bowl at right, similar to the *dari* in shape, was made on the island of Espiritu Santo in New Hebrides, where the potter's art survives in two villages. Pottery is made and traded among the islands off the eastern end of New Guinea; but the days are past when pots were the stock-in-trade of fleets of *lakatoi* from the villages around Port Moresby on the Southern coast.

*Pottery vessels
in traditional
forms. Fiji.*

Above: Fijian potter making a bowl.
Below: Pottery bowl.
Espiritu Santo, New Hebrides.

81

With a fair wind, the fleet would set sail in September or October, for the Papuan Gulf. There the pots were traded for sago from the sago palms and for timber to refurbish the *lakatoi*. The great sailing vessels each had three or more big log dugouts set side by side to carry the broad deck, and tree trunks were needed to renew the dugouts each year.

Left: Two cooking pots.
Espiritu Santo, New Hebrides.
Right: Pottery vessel. Papua.

Pottery was not a widespread art among the people of the sea. It had died out in Polynesia long before the white men came. In Micronesia, where few islands provided any clay, village potters were active in Yap and Palau until a few years ago, and the island of Guam had a long tradition of fine pottery making, beginning with thin delicate wares nearly 4,000 years old. But the universal material for making beautiful vessels was wood.

Most men with the skill to make a dugout canoe could also shape a simple wooden food bowl. Only the master artist, rigorously trained, could carve a temple image or the prow of a sacred canoe, or make a bowl for the solemn ritual of kava. From the hands of these men came some of the greatest works of island art.

Fleet of lakatoi
*setting sail from Mailu,
Papua New Guinea, 1927.*

7

Wood
for the
Master
Artist—
I

The making of a kava bowl, simple in form and without decoration, is important work for the wood-carvers of Fiji, Tonga, and Samoa. In the past, and still today, the kava bowl is the center of a solemn and impressive ceremony. No meeting of chiefs or welcome of guests to a village is complete without the drinking of kava, and it is an honor to receive a cup from the bowl of a high chief. The bowl above was a famous one, belonging to Cakobau, the last king of Fiji, who ceded the islands to Queen Victoria in 1874. When the kava was served to guests, the sennit cord attached to the bowl would be stretched toward the man of highest rank, to whom the first cup of kava was presented.

Some of the best-known makers of kava bowls in Fiji are the wood-carvers of Kabara in the Lau Islands, also the home of skilled makers of tapa.

Opposite: Shaping a kava bowl with an adze. Kabara, Lau Islands, Fiji.
Above: King Cakobau's kava bowl. Fiji, 19th century.

The bowl and its legs should be carved from one block of wood. Here we see a man of Kabara beginning to shape the block with an axe. The rounded top is then hollowed out with firm strokes of the adze. (See page 84.) The four-legged bowl, still unfinished, is shown opposite, with the simple tools of the carver.

First stage in making a kava bowl. Kabara, Lau Islands, Fiji.

Kava bowls of similar shape are also made in Samoa. There, as in Fiji, the preparation of the drink in the bowl is part of the ritual. Kava is made by mixing water with the dried root of a pepper plant. In a Samoan village this is a traditional task of the *taupou*, the daughter of the highest chief. Wearing a tall headdress, like the one on page 62, the *taupou* sits on the floor of the big round meetinghouse of the village and vigorously strains the liquid in the bowl through a bundle of hibiscus fibers. The chiefs assembled for the ceremony sit cross-legged with their backs against the pillars that support the domed roof of the house. When the kava is ready, one of the chiefs calls out the names and titles of those who are to drink. A coconut-shell cup of kava is carried to each man in turn, to be drained at a single draft and handed back to the cupbearer.

Roughly finished bowl (center) with Kabara carver's tools.

Above: Boat-shaped food bowl.
Austral Islands.
Below: Chief's stool. Tahiti.

On the islands of eastern Polynesia, even in the past, no ceremony surrounded the kava bowl and the drinking of kava, but master artists created wonderful wood-carved furnishings for the households of chiefs. In a world where everyone sat on the floor, high chiefs in Tahiti were enthroned on elegant stools. As a symbol of his prestige and power, a chief would carry a large sennit fly whisk with a delicately carved wooden handle. He would also use a fine woven fan, like the one at the bottom of page 41.

Chief's fly whisk with carved handle. Tahiti.

Many different styles of art in wood developed in the scattered island groups of Polynesia, even though the Polynesians were essentially one people, whether they lived in Hawaii, Tahiti, or New Zealand. In the islands of Melanesia, with their widely varied peoples, customs, and languages, the artists produced a still greater variety of wood-carved art.

A feast bowl made in the Admiralty Islands, off the north coast of New Guinea, has four short legs and two graceful handles of carved openwork. Another bowl, from the eastern Solomons, is inlaid with shell and carved in the form of a frigate bird holding a fish. This type of bowl was used for ritual food offerings to the gods and the ancestral spirits of the island fishermen.

Large food bowl for feasts.
Marquesas Islands.

*Above: Ceremonial food bowl
nearly 5 feet long. Admiralty Islands.
Below: Bowl for ritual
offerings. Solomon Islands.*

The canoe house by the beach is the center of art and life for the men of the eastern Solomons. The finest wood-carvers work in the canoe house, making offering bowls and the fishing floats used to catch flying fish. Above all, they build and decorate the bonito canoes.

Old tradition says that the bonito, the noblest of fish, are sent by the gods, and their coming is a sign that the gods are well pleased with the people. Therefore, the bonito canoes are sacred vessels, enriched with all the skill of the carver. They wait in the canoe house until the great day when the bonito schools appear offshore, attended by flocks of seabirds. Then the canoes are carried down to the sea, and the men go out to troll for the fish with their lures of shining shell.

Left: Carved fishing float.
Right: Carving for the prow
of a bonito canoe. Both from
Eastern Solomon Islands.

Their work is dangerous, for they must compete against the sharks, which also prey on the bonito. Sharks have always played a large part in the lives of the sea people. In the eastern Solomons they were more often allies than enemies. The souls of successful bonito fishermen were said to live on in the bodies of sharks.

Launching a sacred bonito canoe.
Eastern Solomon Islands.

On the island of Ulawa, each landing place was guarded by a shark that would come to the people's help. And on the Santa Cruz Islands, men worshiped a shark spirit, represented by a small wooden figure like the one above.

Everywhere among the island peoples, fishermen invoked gods and spirits to help them in their work. The little Polynesian tiki at the left, with hands clasping its stomach, is a "fishing god" from Rarotonga in the Cook Islands, where the fishermen used to carry these figures aboard their canoes to bring them a good catch.

Left: "Fisherman's god." Rarotonga, Cook Islands. Right: Figure of a shark spirit. Santa Cruz Islands.

The art of the wood-carver could also provide strong magical protection against storm and shipwreck for men on long voyages between the islands.

The two little figures in the center of this canoe-prow carving are the magical protectors of the canoe and are said to come alive at sea. The carving was made in the Trobriand Islands, off the eastern end of New Guinea, where the people are famous for their seafaring and their artistry in wood. There the canoes for trading voyages, not for fishing, demand the skill of the best carvers. The people say today, as in the past, that the most important work for a carver is the making of *lagim*, the splashboards for the prow and stern of a trading canoe.

The carving above is the top part of a *lagim* for the prow of a canoe. The curving wings at the sides, called butterflies by the carvers, are never made symmetrical. On the prow, the larger wing is at the right, facing toward the outrigger; on the stern, at the left. The stylized forms of snakes, birds, fish and snails are worked into the spiraling design of the *lagim*, according to the taste and skill of the carver.

Top of a lagim—splashboard
for the prow of a canoe.
Trobriand Islands.

95

Lagim *for the stern of*
a canoe. *Trobriand Islands.*

96

An image of the white heron is usually included in the carving of the *tabuya*, the board that is fitted against the *lagim*. The Trobriand people say that the heron is the most graceful of all birds, a creature of perfect balance.

The carvers of *lagim* make each one different, and only the finest artists have the quality the people call *sope*. This literally means "water"; but in art it stands for rhythm, a free flow of design, and also for the artist's knowledge of the meaning and magic of the symbols he carves. A fine *lagim* can be so expressive that it seems to spring to life when the canoe is launched in the sea. The people see it then as the face of a living human being, no longer the work of the carver's hand.

Tabuya—*carving for the prow of a canoe.*

97

Canoes for fishing and trading were not the only vessels to be built and decorated by the best artists. War canoes of the past were equally splendid examples of the carver's art.

The long black *tomoko* canoes of the western Solomons, as we have seen, were made beautiful with shell inlay and with borders of white cowries on the high upstanding prows. The *tomoko* also carried a magical protector, the carved spirit figure lashed to the canoe prow at the waterline. These sculptures, called *gnuzugnu-zu*, were peculiar to the Solomon Islands. The carvers followed a strict convention but still managed to vary the form. The figure at the right holds a second figure in its hands, and its shell inlay is particularly fine.

Prow of a tomoko canoe.
Vella Lavella, Solomon Islands.

98

War was a way of living for the men who went out on head-hunting raids in the *tomoko* canoes. The art and craftsmanship of these canoes arose from the needs of warriors in a violent world. Wars and skirmishes were common among the island peoples, especially in the later days of their history, just before the coming of the white men. By then, the population of the islands had increased, and powerful chiefs rose up in rivalry.

Spirit carving for
the prow of a canoe.
Malaita, Solomon Islands.

99

This Hawaiian image portrays a war god in all his violence and ferocity. The figure was set up on a *heiau*, one of the big outdoor places of worship that belonged to the highest chiefs. It has the energy and feeling of movement that make Hawaiian sculptures so different from those of the rest of Polynesia. The marks of the sculptor's adze, plainly visible, give the carving an additional rugged strength, and its rounded muscular form seems to reflect the Hawaiians' love of sport and physical prowess.

Wood sculptures of war gods.
Left: Cook Islands.
Right: Hawaii.

100

In Hawaii, war itself was a kind of sport, pursued at certain seasons and governed by strict rules. Even the war god Ku was not always fierce. He was also the kindly god of the forest, the patron of canoe builders, and the helper of farmers and fishermen.

In New Zealand, disputes over land for farming often led to wars among the Maori. Villages had to be strongly fortified with high stockades, and the people on their guard against attack. Like other island warriors, the Maori fought with weapons that were beautiful to look at, as well as deadly on the field of battle. War could be a terrible destroyer of art, as the shattered statues of Easter Island bear witness; but the needs of the warrior could inspire master artists to create exciting forms, especially when they turned to making weapons.

Head of a war club.
Maori, New Zealand.

8

Wood for the Master Artist— II

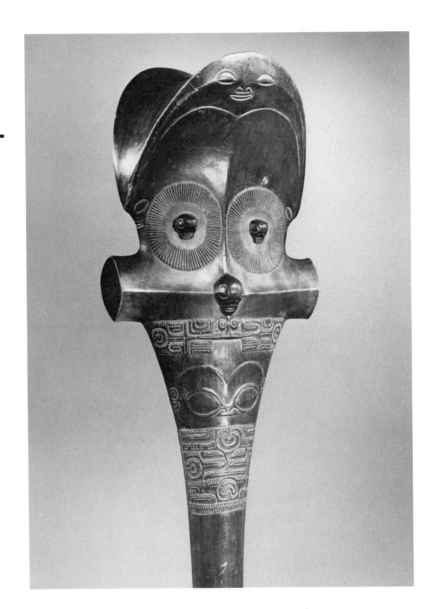

...n island people went to war, one of their favorite weapons
...he wooden club; and the wood-carvers of each island group
... clubs in a different style. Among the most impressive were
...ceremonial clubs of the Marquesas, long-handled and with
...e head carved in a human face design.

In Fiji, where clubs were a major form of art, a chief's club
might take years to make, for it was carved in the living tree and
shaped by the growing form of trunk and branch. The clubs of
famous warriors were known by name, and were believed to pos-
sess the *mana*—the special power—of their owners.

Heads of war clubs.
Opposite: Marquesas Islands.
Above: New Hebrides.

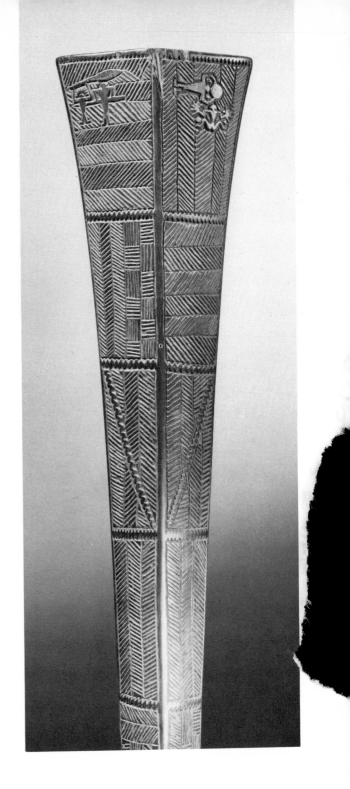

Left: Three war clubs, Fiji.
Right: Top of a war club. Tonga.

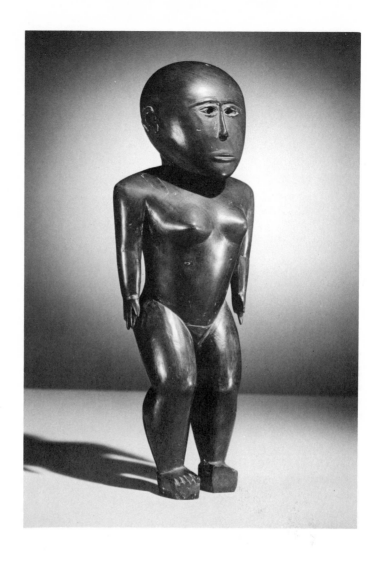

The tall war clubs of Tonga were covered with incised geometric designs, interspersed with tiny carvings of men and animals.

The fighting chiefs of Tonga, who carried these elegant weapons, also kept in their houses small wooden sculptures of goddesses, as beautifully finished as the clubs. These little figures were made only in Tonga and seem to be more closely related to the sculptures of Hawaii than to the tiki of eastern Polynesia.

Small figure of
a goddess. Tonga.

The stone-bladed adze of the carver was never used as a weapon of war; but among the Maori, incomparable carvers of wood, it became a symbol of power. When a chief addressed his people, he would hold in his hand a ceremonial adze with a sculptured handle.

Common everyday things were also richly adorned by the Maori artists. The knife opposite, edged with shark's teeth, was a practical tool for cutting meat at feasts. Yet the maker turned it into a thing of beauty, working the wooden haft into the spiral design that we see so often in Maori art.

Above: Ceremonial adze of Maori chief.
Opposite: Knife with cutting edge
of shark's teeth. Maori.

This figure sculpture, also decorated with spirals, probably re-presented an ancestor, a famous Maori warrior of days gone by. When his image was mounted on the top of a village stockade, the people believed that the ancestral spirit would help to defend them against their enemies.

Belief in the power of the dead to help the living was common among the island peoples. The heroes of the past were still alive to their descendants. Their stories were passed down from generation to generation, and in Polynesia the greatest heroes might eventually become gods.

Ancestor figure with facial tatu. Maori.

The tall, thin image at the right, from the Cook Islands, is said to show Rongo, the god of farmers, and his three sons. Wooden figures of gods like this one were not considered sacred in themselves but simply served as dwelling places for the spirits of the gods, called down by priests at times of festival or of special need.

In Melanesia, gods, ancestors, and other supernatural beings were often invoked through masked dancing, as we have seen. If the carver made a good mask, the spirit would enter it; and when the mask was worn by a dancer and moved in the patterns of the dance, the spirit became a living being.

Left: Painted mask. Papua New Guinea.
Right: Figure sculpture. Cook Islands.

109

The mask opposite is one of the spectacular carvings made for the Malanggan Ceremony, which follows the death of an important person on the island of New Ireland. Masks of this kind represent people who have died, some recently and some in the distant past.

The small carving at the left was also worn in dance, hanging around the neck of the dancer. An ancestor figure from Easter Island, it is totally different in style from the stone giants of the *ahu* and unlike any other sculpture of Polynesia. Little is known about these figures. Many were made by the artists of Easter Island, and all of them look emaciated, like a corpse. The bodies curve in the form of the small pieces of wood from which they were carved. Wood was scarce on that island of stone, and these were precious objects, treasured by their owners.

Above: Figure sculpture. Easter Island.
Opposite: Mortuary mask. New Ireland.

110

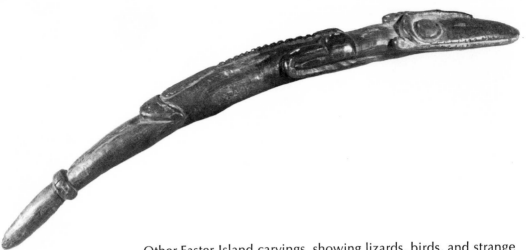

Other Easter Island carvings, showing lizards, birds, and strange creatures, half man and half animal, remind us of the close ties between men and the animal world. Ancient traditions of the island peoples often trace back families to an animal ancestor, rather than a human being. To have a shark for an ancestor could be a source of pride and thankfulness, for it meant one had a kinship with sharks and need not fear them.

We see a blending of the forms of man and crocodile on an ancestor board from the Papuan Gulf. These carved and painted memorials to the dead, each bearing a different design, were preserved in the village meetinghouses of the men, where masks were made and holy things kept hidden.

*Carved lizard and
bird. Easter Island.*

The bird carving from Easter Island is probably a sooty tern, the sacred bird of the creator god Make Make and the center of the Birdman festival. Every spring, the people of the island would gather at the village of Orongo, perched high above the sea, the place of rock-cut pictures of bird-headed men. From there the servants of the chiefs would swim out to the rocky islet of Motu-nui, where the terns nested and where the men were to wait for the laying of the first egg. The one to find the egg would shout his triumph from a high rock called The Cry of the Bird. Then he would swim back with the egg through the rough and shark-infested sea, and his master would be appointed Birdman for a year, a sacred being living in seclusion and receiving tributes of food from the people.

Everyone rejoiced after the festival. The return of Make Make's birds to their nesting island was a sign of the god's blessing and a promise that land and sea would give the people food for another year.

Shortage of food was a constant threat to many of the people of the sea. Life was not easy for island farmers. They needed the help of the spirits that ruled over water, weather, and the fertility of the soil.

Ancestor board.
Papuan Gulf.

113

These three spirit masks take us from the big island of New Caledonia, where the hook-nosed water spirits danced in their black feathered costumes, to small islands of Micronesia and the Torres Strait.

The rare Micronesian mask, from the Mortlock Islands, was worn for a ceremonial dance on the beach to protect the breadfruit trees against typhoons, the terrible storms that could strip the low islands of all life.

The mask from Saibai Island in the Torres Strait was made for a joyful autumn festival after the harvest of wild plums had been safely gathered in. This mask probably represented one of the good spirits that had brought the rich harvest and given the people a cause to celebrate with feasting, dance, and song.

Opposite: Water-spirit mask.
New Caledonia.
Above left: Mask for dance protecting
breadfruit trees. Mortlock Islands.
Above right: Harvest festival mask.
Saibai, Torres Strait.

115

The joys of a feast, with food in plenty and to spare, are reflected in the art of the wood-carvers, the makers of splendid food bowls large and small.

The covered bowl above, carved in the form of a bird and inlaid with shell, is from the Palau Islands in Micronesia. The Palauans have a long and proud tradition of fine wood carving. Their green islands, where the people of Yap used to come to quarry limestone, supply plenty of timber for the carver and builder, and the Palauan artists have developed an art that is uniquely their own. Many wood-carvers, as we have seen, produced designs with symbolic or magical meaning; only the carvers of Palau told stories in wood and created buildings whose decorations could be read like a book.

These buildings, the supreme achievements of Palauan art, were the *bai*, the council houses of village elders and centers of life for the men. Few *bai* survive today, although there are men in Palau with the knowledge and skill to build them.

Bowl in the form of a bird.
Palau, Caroline Islands.

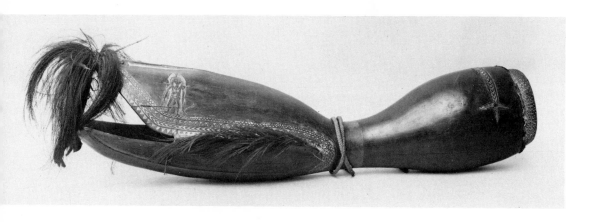

Above: Drum. Saibai,
Torres Strait.
Below: Bowl, probably
for holding salt. Hawaii.

A *bai* was built on a monumental scale, of heavy interlocking timbers. Its four great corner posts stood for the four chief clans of the village, and the doorposts at either end symbolized the four most important women. But the glory of the *bai* was in the storytelling pictures, carved in low relief and painted in earth colors—ochre, black, white, yellow, and red.

On the planks of the high gables was a record of the myths and history of the village, displayed for all to see. The telling of lesser tales continued on the tie beams that stretched across the great hall inside, above the polished floor where the elders took their seats for solemn meetings.

Above and opposite: Interior and exterior of a traditional bai—*men's meetinghouse. Palau.*

118

At times of celebration, the whole village would gather at the *bai*, and a feast would be served to hundreds of guests.

Here, in a painting by the Palauan artist Charles Gibbons, we see two village *bai* in the midst of all the bustle of preparation for a feast. Men and women bring in the food from the gardens and the sea—pigs and fish and baskets of taro. More taro roots are piled on racks, ready to be given away to the guests, and the tall wooden vat in the center will be filled with a sweet drink of coconut syrup and water.

Men are seated against the stone backrests on the paved platform around the *bai*, and high above their heads rise the storytelling gables with their pictures of sharks and triggerfish, a fishnet, a canoe, and a fight with spears. In this painting the artist looks back to remembered scenes of his boyhood and to tales of long ago. He creates a vision of the old culture of Palau, as it was before the white men had invaded the world of the Pacific islanders.

Gibbons' pictures, like windows, show us in rich detail a pattern of living in which each person had a place. Here not only the wood-carvers, who built and decorated the great *bai*, but all artists and craftsmen were important and necessary members of society. The coming of the white men destroyed this ancient, well-ordered world.

While old arts and old ways persist in some parts of the Pacific, the island artists of today cannot ignore the changed conditions of life and the new influences that crowd in on them. Their art must change, and new ways must be found to express new ideas.

Opposite: Preparations for a feast in a Palauan village.
Painting by Charles Gibbons, Palau.

9

New Art
from the Old

The canoes of the Pacific peoples, in all their varied forms, have been our guides in tracing the story of island art. Designed as wonderfully seaworthy vessels, they also expressed the faith and beliefs of their makers and symbolized a whole way of living.

The building of a canoe was a sacred act, watched over by the gods. The realm of gods and spirits was close to the human world, and the gods themselves were said to be travelers in canoes.

This painting by Charles Gibbons shows a Palauan racing canoe sailing among the wooded islets off the main island shore. According to an old myth, the gods came to Palau in swift canoes like this one, and were as fond of canoe racing as the Palauan chiefs. Today, these slender craft are no more than a memory. The artist delineates carefully the graceful curved hull, which was always carved from a single tree trunk; the attachment of the outrigger; and the sail made from many strips of matting.

Opposite: Palauan racing canoe.
Painting by Charles Gibbons, Palau.
Above: Outrigger canoe in
Ponape Lagoon, Caroline Islands.

123

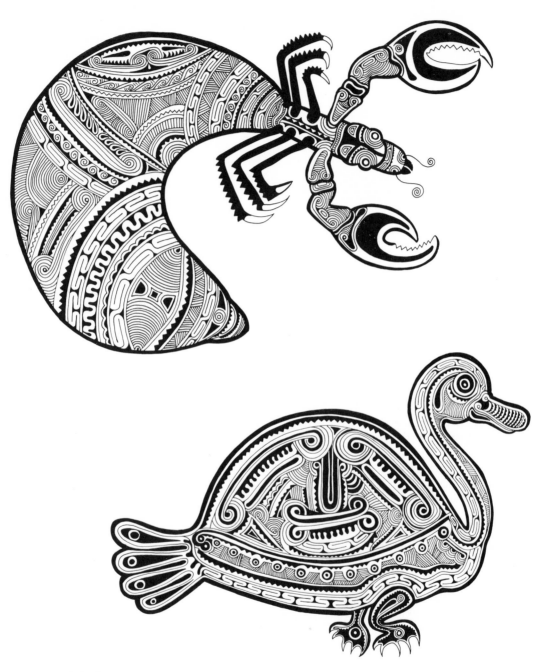

Lobster and duck.
Drawings by Martin Morububuna,
Trobriand Islands.

Charles Gibbons of Palau is one of a growing company of new artists, scattered about the island world of the people of the sea. He was a wood-carver in the Palauan tradition before he began, late in life, to paint scenes from the vanishing past of his people. Though he used the medium of watercolor, foreign to island artists, the flat pattern of his pictures links them with the old Palauan storytelling art, the painted reliefs of the *bai*.

Martin Morububuna is from the Trobriand Islands in Papua New Guinea. His people are famous for their artistry in wood and especially for the splendid decoration of their canoes. The flowing rhythms of the wood-carved designs have found fresh expression in the ink drawings of Morububuna. Working freehand with a pen instead of the tools of the carver, he has developed his own style of drawing, strongly rooted in the art of his ancestors.

Wooden spatula for lime, used in chewing betelnut. Trobriand Islands.

125

Other Pacific artists have turned to painting in oils. They have explored abstract design or observed with a painter's eye the people and landscape of their islands. The work of Adriano Pangelinan, a painter of Guam, reflects what has changed in the lives of the islanders, but also what is eternally the same. In a pen-and-ink study of the rocky shore, he evokes in a few delicate lines that ever-present reality of island life—the limits of the land and the vastness of the encircling sea.

These new artists of the South Pacific are pioneers like their ancestors, the bold navigators who made the sea their highway in the search for new land. The ancestors carried with them memories of their old homes and of the arts, skills, and wisdom of their people. The artists of today remember and take increasing pride in their ancient island heritage. As they create new arts from the old, the story we have followed in this book moves on, like a voyage of discovery, into an unknown future.

Above and opposite:
Drawings by
Adriano Pangelinan, Guam.

List of Illustrations

Measurements are in centimeters.
Bold number indicates book page.

i Stopper for gourd lime container. Wood. Santa Cruz Islands, Solomon Islands. Height: 6.8 cm. Courtesy Field Museum of Natural History, Chicago.

ii Detail of one end of a carrying pole. Wood. Hawaii. Length of pole: 160 cm. Courtesy Field Museum of Natural History, Chicago.

v Ceremonial sword. Wood inlaid with pearl shell. Palau, Caroline Islands. The British Museum.

vi Drum. Wood, skin. Papuan Gulf, Papua New Guinea. Length: 88.75 cm. The British Museum.

vii Lime container (used when chewing betelnut). Gourd. Trobriand Islands, Papua New Guinea. Height: 23 cm. The British Museum.

x *A Canoe of the Sandwich Islands, the Rowers Masked, 1777.* Engraving from painting by John Webber. *Cook's Third Voyage, Atlas*, Plate 65. Photo: Bernice P. Bishop Museum.

1 Dolphin. Wood inlaid with pearl shell. Ulawa, Eastern Solomon Islands. Length: 105.5 cm. The British Museum.

3 *Lakatoi* under sail, Port Moresby, Papua New Guinea. Photo: J. W. Lindt, 1885. La Trobe Collection, State Library of Victoria, Melbourne.

4 Canoe of Rongelab, Marshall Islands. Photo: Courtesy American Museum of Natural History.

5 Stick chart. Pandanus root, cowrie shells, fiber. Utric Atoll, Marshall Islands. Courtesy American Museum of Natural History.

6 Sailing canoe, Tahiti. Drawing by Lieut. G. Tobin, 1792. Photo: Bernice P. Bishop Museum.

7 *Boats of the Friendly Islands* (Tonga). From a painting by John Webber, published in London in 1809. Photo: Bernice P. Bishop Museum.

8 Canoe bailer. Wood. Maori, New Zealand. Courtesy Field Museum of Natural History, Chicago.

9 Working adze. Wood, stone, coconut fiber. Tahiti. Length: 50.5 cm. Courtesy Field Museum of Natural History, Chicago.

10 Wood-carver of Palau, Caroline Islands, working with an adze. Photo: The Palau Museum.

11 Tackle box. Wood inlaid with shell. Gilbert Islands. The Fiji Museum.

12 Detail of interior of plank-built canoe, showing how ribs are lashed to cleats in the planks. Ulawa, Eastern Solomon Islands. The British Museum.

13 *Tomoko* (war canoe) and canoe house; slits in front wall of house to accommodate high prows of canoes. Roviana Lagoon, New Georgia, Western Solomon Islands. The British Museum. Photo: C. M. Woodford, first Resident Commissioner for British Solomon Islands.

14 Detail of roof construction; beams of house bound together with sennit. Gilbert Islands. Photo: W. K. Curtis.

15 Building a canoe; lashing together the planks with sennit. Gilbert Islands. Photo: W. K. Curtis.

16 Masthead of *ndrua* (large double canoe). Wood. Fiji. The Fiji Museum.

17 Fijian *ndrua*. Photo: Courtesy American Museum of Natural History.

18 Trading canoe with traditional matting sails. Siassi Islands, Papua New Guinea. Photo: Philip J. C. Dark.

20-21 Dancers performing the *Mit-Mit*, traditional dance by which one village honors another. Village of Kanif, Dalipebanau Municipality, Yap, Caroline Islands. Photo: United Nations.

22 Dancers dressed for the *Mit-Mit*. Village of Kanif, Yap. Photo: United Nations.

23 Detail of end of lavalava (woman's skirt) woven in *Metchi*, the traditional "king's pattern." Banana fiber, dyed black, blue and red. Fais, Western Caroline Islands. Full size of skirt: 152 cm. x 54 cm. Courtesy Peabody Museum of Salem. Photo: Maureen Liacos.

24 Men performing a *meke*. Fiji. Photo: Ministry of Information, Fiji.

25 Feather masks. Awar, Papua New Guinea. Photo: Courtesy Field Museum of Natural History, Chicago.

26 *A Man of the Sandwich Islands, with His Helmet, 1784.* Engraving from work by John Webber. *Cook's Third Voyage, Atlas*. Photo: Bernice P. Bishop Museum.

27 *Kahili* (feathered scepter). Feathers, wood. Hawaii. Height: 135 cm. Courtesy Peabody Museum of Salem. Photo: M. W. Sexton.

28 Cloak. Woven fiber, feathers. Hawaii. University Museum, University of Pennsylvania.

29 Cloak. Feathers, fiber. Maori, New Zealand, about 1910. UCLA Museum of Cultural History. Photo: Susan Einstein.

30 Maori council house with Maori people in traditional and European dress. New Zealand, about 1900. Photo: Courtesy Peabody Museum of Salem.

31 Cloak. Flax. Maori, New Zealand. Courtesy Field Museum of Natural History, Chicago.

32 Detail of *taniko* border of flax cloak. Maori, New Zealand. UCLA Museum of Cultural History. Photo: Susan Einstein.

33 Vessel for pouring. Engraved gourd. Maori, New Zealand. Bernice P. Bishop Museum.

34-35 Cloak with stripes of woven flax and *taniko*. Maori, New Zealand, 1850–60. UCLA Museum of Cultural History. Photo: Susan Einstein.

36 Body armor. Sennit, sharkskin. Gilbert Islands. Courtesy Peabody Museum of Salem.

37 Weaver with backstrap loom. Ulithi, Western Caroline Islands. Photo: The Palau Museum.

38 Woven sash. Banana fiber, wool embroidery and fringe, white shell disks, glass beads. Ponape, Caroline Islands, about 1830. 167 cm. x 8.8 cm. Courtesy Peabody Museum of Salem. Photo: Maureen Liacos.

39 Woven sash. Banana fiber, wool. Kosrae, Caroline Islands. 162 cm. x 8 cm. Courtesy Peabody Museum of Salem. Photo: Maureen Liacos.

40 Detail of corner of woven mat. Pandanus fiber. Joluit, Marshall Islands. Size of mat: 81 cm. x 82 cm. Courtesy Peabody Museum of Salem. Photo: Maureen Liacos.

41 (Top) Fan. Pandanus fiber with turtle shell center. Marshall Islands. Height: 37.25 cm. Collection Castleton State College, Vermont. Photo: James Barker.

(Bottom) Fan. Plaited coconut leaflets, hardwood handle. Society Islands (Tahiti). Height: 45 cm. Otago Museum, Dunedin, New Zealand.

42 Painted tapa (bark cloth). Austral Islands. Length: 240 cm. Courtesy Peabody Museum of Salem.

43 Mask. Bark cloth on wickerwork base. Papuan Gulf, Papua New Guinea. Height: 38.75 cm. The British Museum.

44 Presentation tapa. Lakeba, Lau Islands, Fiji, 1957. Photo: Ministry of Information, Fiji.

45 Two details of painted tapa. Samoa. Courtesy Field Museum of Natural History, Chicago.

46 (Left) *Kupesi* (tablet with relief design for making patterns on tapa). Pandanus leaves and ribs of coconut fronds. Fiji. 50 cm. x 23.75 cm. Courtesy Peabody Museum of Salem. Photo: Maureen Liacos.

(Right) detail of tapa design made with *kupesi* and accented with painting. Tonga. Size of tapa: 47.5 cm. x 36.25 cm. Collection Castleton State College, Vermont. Photo: James Barker.

47 Tapa with design made by stencils and *kupesi*. Kabara, Lau Islands, Fiji. 155 cm. x 180 cm. Collection Castleton State College, Vermont. Photo: James Barker.

48 Tapa masks. Papuan Gulf, Papua New Guinea. Photo: Courtesy Field Museum of Natural History, Chicago.

49 Maori with facial tatu. New Zealand. Photo: Courtesy Peabody Museum of Salem.

50 Wooden arm carved with examples of tatu designs. Marquesas Islands. Length: 61 cm. Courtesy Peabody Museum of Salem.

51 Tattooed man of Nukuhiva, Marquesas Islands. Engraving from Langsdorf, *Voyages around the World, I, 1803–1807.* Published 1813. Photo: Courtesy American Museum of Natural History.

52 (Top) Man's chest tatu. Bellona, Solomon Islands.

(Bottom) Man's body tatu. Sonsorol, Western Caroline Islands.

53 (Top) Tools of the tatu artist. Fiji. (Left) Length: 20.4 cm. (Right) Length: 22.2 cm. Courtesy Field Museum of Natural History, Chicago.

(Bottom) Woman's hand tatu. Ponape, Eastern Caroline Islands.

54 Two composite fishhooks. Whalebone shank faced with shell, turtle shell point, fiber bindings. Tonga. Courtesy Field Museum of Natural History, Chicago.

55 (Left) Fishhook. Turtle shell, twelve brown beads. Ponape, Caroline Islands.

(Right) Composite fishhook. Bone, turtle shell, feather lure, fiber bindings. Tobi, Caroline Islands. Length: 16.5 cm. Both: Courtesy Peabody Museum of Salem. Photos: Maureen Liacos.

56 (Top left) Composite fishhook. Marshall Islands. Length: 8 cm.

(Lower left) Fishhook. Pearl shell. Nukuoro, Caroline Islands. 5.5 cm. x 4.8 cm. Both: Courtesy Peabody Museum of Salem. Photos: Maureen Liacos.

(Right) Three breast ornaments. Solomon Islands. (Above) Two disks. Giant clamshell with turtle shell overlay. Florida and Santa Cruz Islands. (Below) Crescent-shaped pendant. Pearl shell with turtle shell overlay. North Malaita. The British Museum.

57 Men dressed as chorus singers for dance. Santa Cruz Islands. University Museum, University of Pennsylvania. Photo: William Davenport.

58 (Top) Ear ornaments. Bone. Marquesas Islands. Length: 4.5 cm. Courtesy Field Museum of Natural History, Chicago.

(Bottom) Headband. Fiber, pearl shell disk with turtle shell overlay. Marquesas Islands. Diam. of shell: 14.8 cm. Courtesy Peabody Museum of Salem.

59 Fish mask. Turtle shell, lime inlay, cassowary plumes. Mabuiag, Western Torres Strait. Length: 125 cm. The British Museum.

60 Mourning costume. Shell, fiber, feathers, tapa. Tahiti. Bernice P. Bishop Museum.

61 Funerary mask. Turtle shell, hair. Mer, Eastern Torres Strait. Height: 40 cm. The British Museum.

62 (Left) Shell money in the form of an arm-ring, decorated with hornbill design. Choiseul, Western Solomon Islands.

(Right) *Taupou* headdress for kava ceremony. Shell, feathers, hair. Samoa. Bernice P. Bishop Museum.

63 (Left) Grave ornament with openwork carving of human figures. Giant clamshell. New Georgia, Western Solomon Islands. Width: 25 cm. The British Museum.

(Right) Ceremonial shield. Wickerwork covered with resin, inlaid wiith pearl shell. Central Solomon Islands, possibly Guadalcanal. Length: 87 cm. The British Museum.

64 Stone money. Yap, Caroline Islands. Photo: United Nations.

66 Ruins of the palace city of Nan Matol, Ponape, Caroline Islands. Photo: United Nations.

67 Stone images outside the crater of Rano Raraku, Easter Island. Photo: James P. Chapin, Crocker Pacific Expedition, January 19, 1935. Courtesy American Museum of Natural History.

68-69 Stone images outside the crater of Rano Raraku, Easter Island. Photo: James P. Chapin, 1935. Courtesy American Museum of Natural History.

69 (Right) Petroglyph showing birdman. Orongo, Easter Island.

70 Image called *Hoa hake hapa ia* (Waves Breaking). Stone. Orongo, Easter Island (collected in 1868). Height: 250.6 cm. The British Museum.

71 *Hei-tiki* (pendant). Nephrite inlaid wiith shell. Maori, New Zealand. Height: 21.5 cm. Courtesy Field Museum of Natural History, Chicago.

72 Double (male-female) tiki. Stone. Hivaoa Island, Marquesas. Height: 10.5 cm. The Brooklyn Museum, A. Augustus Healy Fund.

73 Stone tiki, still in original place, half-hidden by jungle growth. Marquesas Islands. Photo: Courtesy American Museum of Natural History.

74 Preliminary shaping of Fijian pot with wooden paddle. Photo: Ministry of Information, Fiji.

75 Three stages in making a Fijian pot. (Right) Cylindrical shape, (center) closed globular shape with hole in side, (left) completed pot ready for firing. Photo: Ministry of Information, Fiji.

76 (Top) Fijian potters making the first cylindrical form and shaping it with paddle and anvil.

(Bottom) Cutting the hole in the side of the pot. Both photos: Ministry of Information, Fiji.

77 Potter using the hole in the clay form when working with paddle and anvil. Photo: Ministry of Information, Fiji.

78 Fijian potter forming the lip of the pot. Photo: Ministry of Information, Fiji.

79 Pottery water jar with spout at side, used in mixing kava. From temple in Rewa District, Viti Levu, Fiji, early 19th century. The Fiji Museum.

80 Four pottery vessels. Fiji. Heights: (Left) 21.9 cm. (Top) 16.9 cm. (Right) 10.6 cm. (Bottom) 11.9 cm. The British Museum.

81 (Top) Fijian potter shaping a *dari* (bowl). Photo: Ministry of Information, Fiji.

(Bottom) Pottery bowl. Espiritu Santo, New Hebrides. Diam.: 22.5 cm. The British Museum.

82 (Left) Two pottery vessels. Espiritu Santo, New Hebrides. (Left) Height: 13.75 cm. (Right) Diam.: 16.25 cm. The British Museum.

(Right) Pottery vessel. Papua, Papua New Guinea. Height: 26.5 cm. Courtesy Field Museum of Natural History, Chicago.

83 Canoes setting out from Mailu, Papua New Guinea. Photo: Rev. W. J. V. Saville, London Missionary Society, about 1927.

84 Wood-carver beginning to shape a kava bowl with an adze. Kabara, Lau Islands, Fiji. Photo: Ministry of Information, Fiji.

85 Kava bowl of King Cakobau. Viti Levu, Fiji, 19th century. Diam.: 110 cm. The British Museum.

86 Making a kava bowl; shaping block of wood with an axe. Photo: Ministry of Information, Fiji.

87 Roughly shaped kava bowl with two finished bowls in turtle form; carver's adzes in the background. Kabara, Lau Islands, Fiji. Photo: Ministry of Information, Fiji.

88 (Top) Food bowl. Wood. Austral Islands. Length: 44.8 cm. Courtesy Field Museum of Natural History, Chicago.
(Bottom) Chief's stool. Wood. Tahiti. Peabody Museum, Harvard University. Photo: E. P. Orchard.

89 Fly whisk. Wood, sennit. Tahiti. University Museum, University of Pennsylvania.

90 Large food bowl for feasts. Wood. Marquesas Islands, 19th century. Courtesy Peabody Museum of Salem.

91 (Top) Ceremonial food bowl. Wood. Admiralty Islands. 61 cm. x 141 cm. The Brooklyn Museum, A. Augustus Healy Fund.
(Bottom) Bowl for food offerings. Wood inlaid with shell. Ugi, Eastern Solomon Islands. Length: 51 cm. The British Museum.

92 (Left) Carved wooden fishing float.
(Right) Carving for prow of a bonito canoe. Both from Eastern Solomon Islands. University Museum, University of Pennsylvania.

93 Launching a sacred bonito canoe. Eastern Solomon Islands. Photo: William Davenport. University Museum, University of Pennsylvania.

94 (Left) "Fisherman's god." Wood. Rarotonga, Cook Islands.
(Right) Figure of shark spirit. Wood. Temotu, Santa Cruz Islands. Height: 20 cm. Both: The British Museum.

95 Top of *lagim* (carved splashboard) for prow of canoe. Wood. Trobriand Islands, Papua New Guinea. Width: 70 cm. The British Museum.

96 *Lagim* for stern of a canoe. Wood. Trobriand Islands, Papua New Guinea. Height: 83.75 cm. The British Museum.

97 (Left) Arrangement of carvings (*lagim* and *tabuya*) on prow of canoe.
(Right) *Tabuya* (carving for prow of canoe).

Wood. Massim area (Eastern Papua New Guinea). Length: 43.75 cm. The British Museum.

98 Prow of *tomoko* canoe, with spirit-carving in place at the waterline. Wood inlaid with pearl shell. Vella Lavella, Western Solomon Islands. The British Museum.

99 *Gnuzugnuzu* (spirit-carving for prow of canoe). Wood inlaid with pearl shell. Malaita, Solomon Islands. Height: 35 cm. The Fiji Museum, Middenway Collection.

100 (Left) Figure of a deity, probably Rimaroa, god of war. Wood. Rarotonga, Cook Islands. Height: 40 cm. Otago Museum, Dunedin, New Zealand.
(Right) Guardian figure from a *heiau* (sacred enclosure) dedicated to the war god, Ku. Wood. Hawaii. Height of figure: 74.4 cm. The British Museum.

101 Head of *taiaha* (long club). Wood. Feathers. Maori, New Zealand. Total length of club: 158.7 cm. Courtesy Field Museum of Natural History, Chicago.

102 Head of a ceremonial club. Wood. Marquesas Islands. Length of club: 135.8 cm. Courtesy Field Museum of Natural History, Chicago.

103 Heads of two war clubs. Wood. New Hebrides. Lengths: (Left) 79.1 cm. (Right) 79.7 cm. Courtesy Field Museum of Natural History, Chicago.

104 (Left) Three forms of war clubs. Fiji. (Left) Rootstock club, (center) club with spur for breaking skull of enemy, (right) throwing club.
(Right) Head of war club. Wood. Tonga. Length of club: 92.1 cm. Courtesy Field Museum of Natural History, Chicago.

105 Standing figure of a goddess. Wood. Tonga. Height: 37.8 cm. Courtesy Field Museum of Natural History, Chicago.

106 Ceremonial adze. Wood, stone, fiber. Maori, New Zealand. Length: 57.5 cm. Courtesy Field Museum of Natural History, Chicago.

107 Knife. Wood, shark teeth, fiber. Maori, New Zealand. Courtesy Peabody Museum of Salem. Photo: M. W. Sexton.

108 Figure of tiki or ancestor. Wood. Maori, New Zealand. The British Museum.

109 (Left) Mask. Painted wood. Tami Islands, Papua New Guinea. Height: 37.5 cm. The British Museum.

(Right) Figure of god Rongo and three sons. Wood. Aitutaki, Cook Islands. Height: 137.5 cm. Otago Museum, Dunedin, New Zealand.

110 Figure of man, possibly ancestor. Wood. Easter Island. Height: 47 cm. The British Museum.

111 Mortuary mask. Painted wood, fiber. New Ireland. 41 cm. x 34 cm. The Brooklyn Museum.

112 (Top) Club or ceremonial wand in the form of a lizard. Wood. Easter Island. Length: 50 cm.
(Bottom) Figure of a bird. Wood. Easter Island. Length: 37.5 cm. Both: Otago Museum, Dunedin, New Zealand.

113 Ancestor board. Painted wood. Papuan, Gulf, Papua New Guinea. UCLA Museum of Cultural History. Photo: Susan Einstein.

114 Mask. Wood, fiber. New Caledonia. Courtesy American Museum of Natural History.

115 (Left) Mask of good spirit, for ceremony to protect breadfruit trees. Painted wood. Satawan, Mortlock Islands (Micronesia). Courtesy American Museum of Natural History.
(Right) Mask worn to celebrate harvest of wild plums. Painted wood, human hair, fiber. Saibai, Northern Torres Strait. The British Museum.

116 Covered bowl in the shape of a bird. Wood inlaid with shell. Palau, Caroline Islands. The British Museum.

117 (Top) Drum. Wood, skin, fiber. Saibai, Northern Torres Strait. Length: 102.5 cm. The British Museum.
(Bottom) Bowl, probably a salt dish, supported by three human figures. Wood. Hawaii. Height: 20 cm. The British Museum.

118 Interior of *bai* (men's meeting hall) constructed on the grounds of the Palau Museum, Koror. Photo: Tom Fisher for Palau Museum.

119 The Palau Museum *bai* (destroyed by a typhoon, April, 1976). Photo: The Palau Museum.

120 Preparations for a feast in front of two *bai* in a Palauan village. Watercolor painting by Charles Gibbons, Palau. Collection C. Price. Photo: James Barker.

122 Palauan sailing canoe. Watercolor painting by Charles Gibbons, Palau. Collection C. Price. Photo: James Barker.

123 Traditional Micronesian outrigger canoe in Ponape Lagoon, Caroline Islands. Photo: United Nations.

124 (Top) Lobster.
(Bottom) Duck. Both: Ink drawings by Martin Morububuna, Trobriand Islands, Papua New Guinea. Collection C. Price. Photos: James Barker.

125 Lime spatula. Trobriand Islands, Papua New Guinea. UCLA Museum of Cultural History. Photo: Susan Einstein.

126 Portrait study. Ink drawing by Adriano Pangelinan, Guam. Artist's collection. Photo: James Barker.

127 Rocks and sea. Ink drawing by Adriano Pangelinan, Guam. Artist's collection. Photo: James Barker.

Books for Further Reading

Alberto Cesare Ambesi, *Oceanic Art* (trans. by Rachel Montgomery). Hamlyn Publishing Group, Ltd., London, 1970.

T. Barrow, *Art and Life in Polynesia*. Charles E. Tuttle Co., Rutland, Vt. and Tokyo, 1972.

——, *The Decorative Arts of the New Zealand Maori*. Charles E. Tuttle Co., Rutland, Vt. and Tokyo, 1973.

——, *Maori Wood Sculpture of New Zealand*. Charles E. Tuttle Co., Rutland, Vt. and Tokyo, 1969.

J. Halley Cox with William H. Davenport, *Hawaiian Sculpture*. The University Press of Hawaii, Honolulu, 1974.

Philip J. C. Dark, *Kilenge Life and Art: A Look at a New Guinea People*. Academy Editions, London; St. Martin's Press, New York, 1974.

Roland W. Force and Maryanne Force, *The Fuller Collection of Pacific Artifacts*. Praeger, New York, 1971.

Thomas Gladwin, *East is a Big Bird: Navigation and Logic on Puluwat Atoll*. Harvard University Press, Cambridge, 1970. (Canoes and navigation in Micronesia).

Jean Guiart, *The Arts of the South Pacific* (trans. by Anthony Christie). The Arts of Mankind, edited by André Malraux and Georges Salles. Thames and Hudson, London; Golden Press, New York, 1963.

A. C. Haddon and James Hornell, *Canoes of Oceania*. Bernice P. Bishop Museum Special Publications 27, 28, 29. Reprint (in one vol.) Bishop Museum Press, Honolulu, 1975.

David Lewis, *We, the Navigators: The Ancient Art of Landfinding in the Pacific*. The University Press of Hawaii, Honolulu (paperback ed.), 1975.

Douglas Newton, *Massim: Art of the Massim Area, New Guinea*. The Museum of Primitive Art, New York, 1975. (Includes the Trobriand Islands).

Lee A. Parsons, *Ritual Arts of the South Seas: The Morton D. May Collection*. The St. Louis Art Museum, 1975.

Roslyn Poignant, *Oceanic Mythology*. Paul Hamlyn, Ltd., London, 1967.

Dorota Czarkowska Starzecka and B.A.L. Cranstone, *The Solomon Islanders*. The Trustees of the British Museum, London, 1974.

Robert C. Suggs, *The Hidden Worlds of Polynesia: The Chronicle of an Archaeological Expedition to Nuku Hiva in the Marquesas Islands*. Mentor Books, The New American Library, New York, 1962.

————, *The Island Civilizations of Polynesia*. Mentor Books, The New American Library, New York, 1960.

Jehanne Teilhet, ed., *Dimensions of Polynesia*. Fine Arts Gallery of San Diego, 1973.

Alan Wardwell, *The Sculpture of Polynesia*. The Art Institute of Chicago, 1967.

Index

Italic number indicates illustration